GOSPEL-CENTERED

Fatherhood

SPENCER VALERI

GOSPEL-CENTERED
FATHERHOOD ISN'T SOMETHING
YOU CAN DO ON YOUR OWN.
YOU NEED THE WISDOM
AND POWER OF GOD.

Table of Contents

Introduction

"Daddy, I love it when you smile at me."

In fatherhood, sweet moments like that are a reminder of God's goodness. In those moments, everything seems right in the world, and you are reminded that He has caused His face to shine upon you (Psalm 80:3, 7). But there will be plenty of trying moments as well. Fatherhood brings with it stress, uncertainty, and God-given responsibilities. In those moments of difficulty, the gospel brings hope and encouragement, and it reminds us that real strength can only be found in Christ.

The goal of this booklet is simple: to remind fathers that the gospel should inform how they conduct their lives and how they approach parenting. The gospel isn't just a simple set of facts that you respond to in order to "get saved" and then move on from. Rather, the gospel is the power of God for salvation—both for salvation from the penalty of sin and deliverance from the power of sin (Romans 1:16).

In this booklet, you will find gospel-centered entries dealing with practical issues that most fathers face, such as balancing life's demands, leading and discipling your kids, extending correction, and handling anger. But you'll also find entries focused on the heart work of the gospel, such as practicing self-denial, avoiding idolatry, loving tenderly, and glorifying God. Some of the entries may resonate with you now in your current stage of fatherhood, but some may not resonate with you for years to come—and that's okay. As you progressively grow into the image of Christ, God will continually reveal to you your need for Him. Our hope and prayer is that, through this booklet, you'll see how the gospel impacts each and every step of your fatherhood journey.

After each entry, you'll find related Scripture verses to meditate on, as well as reflection questions for prayer. You are likely busy, so the idea of taking fifteen minutes to read an entry, meditate on Scripture, and journal prayerful responses just might not seem like it is in the cards. But gospel-centered fatherhood isn't something you can do on your own. You need the wisdom and power of God to father like the Father, and that can only come from spending time with Him. God promises us that if we draw near to Him, He will draw near to us (James 4:8). So carve out that time, and "let the word of Christ dwell in you richly" (Colossians 3:16, ESV) before prayerfully answering the questions. May God meet you through these pages and in the day-to-day struggles and joys of fatherhood.

MAY GOD MEET YOU THROUGH

THESE PAGES AND IN THE

DAY-TO-DAY STRUGGLES AND

JOYS OF FATHERHOOD.

No. 01

A Man's Highest Calling

1 Corinthians 10:31

Romans 11:36

Psalm 73:25–26

What is the purpose of man? Why did God create men and women? Perhaps more than ever, people are wrestling with the question of purpose. Society tells us to find our purpose in our net worth, our relationships, our work, or our role as the provider for our families. All of those are good things, but what is the highest calling that God has placed on our lives?

To answer this question, it can be helpful to think of a target face. A target typically has a series of concentric circles with a bullseye in the middle. All of those circles might represent various roles or purposes that God has for men. You might be a father, a husband, an employee, a business owner, or a servant in church. But what is the bullseye? What is the main purpose of man?

We have to look to God's inspired, authoritative Word for that answer. Beginning in the creation account, we can see that God created us with a purpose. Genesis 1:26 tells us of God's plan to create man. He says, "Let us make man in our image, according to our likeness." Then He executes His plan in verse 27: "So God created man in his own image; he created him in the image of God; he created them male and female." People were made, from the beginning, as image-bearers of God.

"Image" is not a term we use very often, but it is closely related to the word "icon." If you pull out your phone, you likely see tons of icons for various apps. Those icons are pictures that are representative of each app. In much the same way, man was created to reflect and represent God here on earth. Through our attitudes and our actions, we are called to display the character of God to those around us.

First Corinthians 10:31 further describes this calling to reflect God to the world; Paul writes, "So, whether you eat or drink, or whatever you do, do everything for the glory of God." That is the main purpose of man. You were created to glorify God. Now, this verse does not tell us to live for the glory of God at the expense of eating and drinking but rather to glorify God *while* eating and drinking. As a man, you still have a calling from God to work hard and to be a godly husband, a loving father, and a selfless servant to others. But your main purpose is to do all those things in a manner that reflects God to those around you and glorifies Him.

Jesus, the God-man, modeled this for us perfectly as He approached His death. He came to earth as the very image of the invisible God (Colossians 1:15), revealing the character of God so that people could see with their own eyes what God was like. Jesus Himself says in John 12:27–28, "Now my soul is troubled. What should I say—Father, save me from this hour? But that is why I came to this hour. Father, glorify your name." The ultimate purpose of Jesus's life was to glorify God. We were made for the same purpose: to exalt God, to reflect Him through all that we do to those around us, and to enjoy Him forever. That is the highest calling of man.

Reflection Questions for Prayer

What have you considered the purpose of your life to be? How has that impacted the way you approach your time, money, and relationships?

As you think about parenting, how can you glorify God through fatherhood?

"

The ultimate purpose of Jesus's life was to glorify God. We were made for the same purpose.

Father Like the Father

John 1:12–13

The highest calling of a man is not fatherhood. Rather, his highest calling is to glorify God. Still, fatherhood is nevertheless a calling and one through which we can glorify God. But how can we glorify God through fatherhood? By reflecting Him.

God is the ultimate example of what it looks like to be a father. Throughout its pages, Scripture shows us how God is the perfect Father. We see that God often refers to His people as His children because they have been adopted into His family. In John 1:12–13, John points out that all believers, because they have received Christ as Lord and Savior, are now called children of God. He writes, "But to all who did receive him, he gave them the right to be children of God, to those who believe in his name, who were born, not of natural descent, or of the will of the flesh, or of the will of man, but of God." Once we come to God through faith, we are adopted into His family and called His children.

It is good for us to think of God as our Father—because He is. As we think about what it means to be a gospel-centered father, it is wise for us to first see how God interacts with His children. The better we understand how God feels about and acts toward His children, the more equipped we will be to father our own children.

So, how do we see God described as a Father in Scripture? Some passages point to the character of God as a Father. In Psalm 103:13, He is described as a Father who shows compassion to His children. In Proverbs 3:12, He is described as a Father who delights in His children. Similarly, Jesus tells us that God is a loving Father when He says, "For the Father himself loves you, because you have loved me and have believed that I came from God" (John 16:27). Other verses describe how the Lord interacts with His children. Proverbs 3:12 also tells us that the Lord disciplines His children when necessary. He is described as a protective Father in Psalm 146:9. In Matthew 7:7–11, Jesus tells a parable indicating that God wishes to give good gifts to His children and to provide for them—all they need to do is ask.

Through these examples and many more, we are given the perfect example of what it looks like to be a father. Our fathering should reflect the fathering we receive from God. So, as we search our hearts and our Bibles in an attempt to be gospel-centered fathers, let us look to God as the greatest Model. The gospel reminds us of the depth of God's love for us. In the ultimate expression of love, Jesus gave up His life for us so that we might be redeemed. If the call to fatherhood is ultimately a call to image and glorify God, then it is also a call to selfless love. It is a call to lay down your life for the sake of those little ones who call you "Daddy" and put their needs above your own, day by day.

Reflection Questions for Prayer

How have you experienced the love of God the Father?

What do you hope your children come to know about the Father's love? How can you be a vessel of that love?

"

Our fathering should reflect the

fathering we receive from God.

Give Yourself Up

John 13:12–15

Luke 9:23

Ephesians 5:25–28

Football on Sunday. Football again on Monday. Motorcycle rides or video games after work. Hanging with friends on Friday night. Fishing and then golfing on Saturday. The list of hobbies that men enjoy is probably endless. Many of us are passionate about our hobbies. They provide us with a sense of relaxation, excitement, creativity, busyness, and in many cases, purpose. Hobbies aren't necessarily a bad thing, but for many of us, hobbies can become consuming, taking our time, energy, and devotion away from our families. Fathers fall short of their calling and problems arise in marriages when these interests take center stage and force family to the sidelines.

The call to gospel-centered fatherhood mirrors the call of the Christian life. It is a call to selflessness—a call to lay down your life for the cause of Christ (Luke 9:23). It is a call to place the needs of your family above your own needs and wants. Gospel-centered fatherhood takes both time and intentionality. In order to disciple your kids and teach them to fear the Lord (Deuteronomy 6), it is likely that you are going to need to sacrifice some of your other pursuits and interests. We will talk about personal interests more in-depth later, but for now, let us think about what it means to love your kids by laying down your life for your family.

Jesus's beloved disciple, John, records an instance in his Gospel where Jesus washed the feet of His disciples. After washing their feet, Jesus says, "So if I, your Lord and Teacher, have washed your feet, you also ought to wash one another's feet. For I have given you an example, that you also should do just as I have done for you" (John 13:14–15). Despite the fact that Jesus was their Lord, He humbled Himself and washed their feet. This showed them the need for His followers to self-sacrificially meet the needs of others. This may seem like a radical call, and by society's standards, it is. But it is the calling of Christ—to consider our children as more important than ourselves.

Christ is calling fathers to consider their children as more important than themselves and to look out for their best interests. As a gospel-centered parent, one of the most important things you can recognize is that your child's greatest need is the gospel. You probably knew from the time your child was six months old that they were sinners. Gospel-centered fatherhood means parenting selflessly—pointing your kids to Christ in both word and action. In this way, your fathering should mirror a Christian's ultimate call: to lay down your own life, hobbies, and passions in order to reflect the hope of the cross for your kids—even when this is easier said than done.

By following the selfless example of Jesus Christ and through the power of the Holy Spirit, you can prioritize your family. It is only through time spent together that you can recognize your child's temptations, sinful tendencies, insecurities, and fears and point them to the hope found in Christ.

Reflection Questions for Prayer

Consider your previous week. How did you spend your free time? How much time did you spend with your family?

What changes could you make in your life to prioritize time with them?

"

_____

Gospel-centered fatherhood
means parenting selflessly —
pointing your kids to Christ
in both word and action.

Being a Bible Man

Colossians 3:16

Ephesians 5:18

We are probably all familiar with the saying "practice makes perfect." It's a phrase we have heard since we were little. It is a common one to hear on little league fields and at soccer practices, but it is even trumpeted by professional athletes, though the elite-level athletes often remind us that *"perfect* practice makes perfect." The whole idea is that diligence and hard work are required to be successful at almost anything we are going to set our minds to do. And many of us have found this to be true in most aspects of our lives. Sure — there may be the occasional thing that you are a "natural" at, but generally, success takes discipline.

Being a father is no different. No one automatically knows how to parent well. Your child is not born one day, and the next, you instantly know all there is to know about fatherhood. But luckily for us as Christian fathers, our diligence does not come from our own strength. God does not ask us to pull ourselves up by our bootstraps. He has given us His Spirit to equip us to walk according to His statutes and help us disciple our children in a way that glorifies Him.

Because the Spirit is essential for growth in godliness—equipping us to walk in His ways—Paul commands us in Ephesians to "be filled by the Spirit" (Ephesians 5:18). Similarly, in Colossians 3:16, Paul instructs the Colossian believers to "let the word of Christ dwell richly" in them. The effects of letting the Word of Christ dwell richly in them are the same as the effects of being "filled by the Spirit" in Ephesians. This suggests that there is a close relationship between letting "the word of Christ dwell richly" and being "filled by the Spirit." God is the One who fills us with His Spirit, but He does so as we dwell in the Word of Christ.

Fatherhood is hard. It can be frustrating. It will push you to your limits. You will lose sleep. You will watch your free time evaporate. There will be days when it will be tempting to work longer hours so that you can avoid the meltdowns that await you at home. These trials cannot be overcome through our own hard work and determination. We need the help of the Spirit. We need to dwell regularly in the Word and allow the Spirit to teach, convict, and empower us to be the fathers that He is calling us to be. As we are filled with the Spirit, our lives will be brought into conformity with the will of God.

Many of us want to be great fathers. We want to be present and engaged with our children. We want to teach them life skills. We want to love them well and teach them to treat others well. But we can only truly disciple our children if we are dwelling in the Word, seeking to do the will of God. No amount of hard work or self-inspired practice will produce "perfect" parenting. But a life devoted to the only One who is perfect can be used to disciple our kids and point them to Christ. May we lean into the Word and seek to be filled by the Spirit so that He might use us as channels of His grace in the lives of our children.

Reflection Questions for Prayer

Think back to when your child was first born. How did you feel? Lost? Confused? Or maybe overwhelmed? How do the truths of the gospel speak to these feelings?

How much time are you spending in the Word? Do you regularly commune with God? How might regular communion with God impact your parenting?

"

God is the One who fills us with
His Spirit, but He does so as we
dwell in the Word of Christ.

You Are Not Alone

John 14:16

1 Corinthians 3:16

Acts 1:8

Galatians 5:16–25

Fatherhood can often seem like a lonely venture. Let's face it: many of us would rather learn the hard way than ask for help. We have all started projects over because we did not want to admit our inadequacies. This stubborn independence carries over into our parenting, and we wind up discouraged and frustrated. Unfortunately, these emotions often express themselves in the form of anger and bitterness.

But God has never intended for man to walk alone. He has always given His people help. In the garden of Eden, God said that it was not good for Adam to be alone, so He made Eve to be his helpmate (Genesis 2:18). Similarly, He has given His people the church body as a community to support one another in their pursuit of Christlikeness. But the greatest helper God has given to His people is the Holy Spirit.

In the days before His ascension, Jesus met with His disciples in the upper room. His disciples were discouraged at the thought of being alone, so Jesus revealed to them that though He would soon leave, He would send them a "Helper," the Holy Spirit (John 14:16, ESV; some versions say "Counselor").

The Spirit now dwells inside all believers and enables us to pursue holiness (Romans 8). We are never alone on our parenting journey. The Spirit is always with us, empowering us to do what Christ has called us to do and helping us to be like Him.

Kids seem to have constant energy. But parents? Not so much. It can be exhausting to come home from a full day at work and then play with busy toddlers for several hours before they finally run out of gas. It can be tempting to crash on the couch instead of engaging with our kids at the end of a long day. But it is hard to intentionally teach, love, and point children toward Christ from the comfort of the couch. In these moments of exhaustion, take heart that God has given us the Spirit, who will empower us to intentionally disciple our children (Ephesians 3:16). He has not left you alone.

Not only does the Spirit strengthen us, but He also equips us to respond to daily difficulties with Christlikeness. Parenting comes with temper tantrums, skinned knees, and broken hearts. When we rely on our strength to respond to these problems, our children are often met with frustration, indifference, and inattentiveness. But the Spirit has not left you alone, and through His help, you can meet these moments with patience, gentleness, and love.

The difference between a sinful response to our children and a response that glorifies God is our dependence on the Spirit. He has not left us alone, but are we relying on Him for strength? Are we walking by the Spirit, trusting that He will produce His fruit in our lives? Or are we walking the road of parenting alone, trusting in our own abilities? May we humbly submit to the Lord and allow His Spirit to help us be the Christ-centered parents we are called to be.

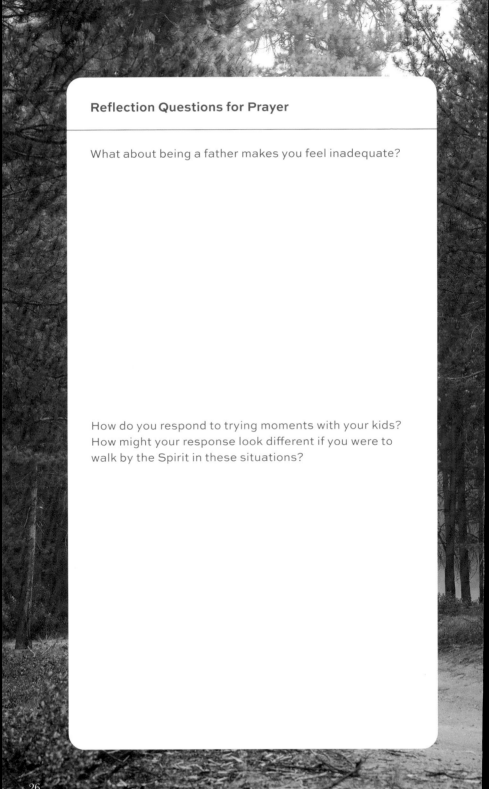

Reflection Questions for Prayer

What about being a father makes you feel inadequate?

How do you respond to trying moments with your kids? How might your response look different if you were to walk by the Spirit in these situations?

"

The difference between a sinful response to our children and a response that glorifies God is our dependence on the Spirit.

Prayer and the Family

Matthew 6:9–13, 7:7–11

For the gospel-centered family, there is no easier and no more powerful pursuit than prayer. Prayer is important for the family. In it, we model for our children our love for God, our dependence upon Him, and our submission to His lordship. In His Sermon on the Mount, Jesus taught His disciples how to pray (Matthew 6:9–13). In this model prayer—also known as the Lord's Prayer—Jesus gives us an example that we can follow as we seek God's face together.

The prayer opens with a focus on worship. Christ acknowledges the closeness and transcendence of God ("Our Father in heaven") before declaring the holiness of God ("your name be honored as holy"). This portion of the prayer is all about Him. When we engage in this type of prayer with our children, we declare to them the glory and majesty of God. Kids have an inherent sense of selfishness. As a father, one of the most important things you can do is remind them that they do not exist for themselves. Rather, they exist for God, who is high and lifted up.

After recognizing the holiness of God, Jesus demonstrates a response of submission to the Father ("Your kingdom come. Your will be done on earth as it is in heaven"). Through these words, Jesus teaches us to not be concerned with accomplishing our own mission; instead, we are to follow His example by asking for God's will to be done. Our response to the character of God indicates a lot about the state of our hearts (1 John 4:8). When we pursue the will of God above our own desires, we are modeling for our children a response of obedience that comes from a heart of love for God, rather than from a place of burden or responsibility.

Our submission to the Father and our response to His character should inform what we need from Him. In the Lord's Prayer, Jesus turns next to the inward needs of the heart ("Give us today our daily bread. And forgive us our debts, as we also have forgiven our debtors"). We have both resource needs and relationship needs. When you pray with your children about needs, you display your neediness. You demonstrate that you do not rely on your own self-sufficiency for provision, and you model the importance of a humble attitude.

This attitude of humility grows from a desire for redemption, both from past guilt and future temptations. In Jesus's last request in this prayer, He asks that God would deliver His people from the evil one. This is a recognition that we are spiritually weak and, therefore, need the power of God to protect us. It's important for our children to realize that we are not all-powerful. Often, they see adults as a strong and safe place—a place where they can hide from the dangers of their imagination. But by demonstrating our trust in the Lord for protection from real evil, we can point them to the only safe place, Jesus.

Prayer forces us to recognize our own weaknesses and turns our hearts to the Lord. When we take time to pray with our children, we let them not only hear but also see our love for God, our dependence upon Him, and our submission to His lordship.

Reflection Questions for Prayer

Do your kids know that you rely on the Lord? How could you show them your reliance on the Lord?

How often do you pray with and for your kids? What are some ways in which you could incorporate prayer into your daily routine?

"

For the gospel-centered family,

there is no easier and no more

powerful pursuit than prayer.

Heart
Idols

Colossians 3:5–6

Have you ever paid much attention to advertising marketed toward men? It's common to see ads including chiseled athletes, scantily clad women, cars or motorcycles, the great outdoors, prominent business leaders, and beautiful homes. This marketing is quite intentional. It tugs at the desires of many men's hearts: status, recreation, women, and entertainment. All of these can be great gifts from God when understood in their proper place, but for many men, they often tug our emotions away from God. When we become so obsessed with our hobbies that we find more enjoyment and satisfaction in them than in God, we have an idol of the heart.

Idols seem to be the culturally appropriate sin of our day, probably because they are an activity of the heart and may not always be observable by our friends and family. Has anyone ever asked you about your obsession with your favorite sports team? Or has anyone ever questioned how often you go golfing while your wife is chasing toddlers around the house? Probably not.

Idolatry is everywhere and can take the form of almost anything: family, work, success, hobbies, sexual desires, or even your favorite sports team or music group. Each of these has the ability to uproot God from the throne of our hearts and pull our affections away from Him. Paul speaks to the danger of idolatry in the book of Colossians: "Therefore, put to death what belongs to your earthly nature: sexual immorality, impurity, lust, evil desire, and greed, which is idolatry. Because of these, God's wrath is coming upon the disobedient" (Colossians 3:5–6).

Because of idolatry, the wrath of God is coming. He will reveal His wrath against those who worship and serve the creation rather than the Creator (Romans 1:25, 2:2). But for those of us in Christ, the old self has already been crucified—the battle has been won. Christ has died for us, making us alive to God and freeing us from our slavery to sin. Paul is urging the Colossian believers not only to believe that truth but to act accordingly. They are not to go on living as though they are still alive to sin when, in reality, they are dead to it. They have been given the power of the Spirit to say "no" to the temptation and comfort of idolatry and put to death idols of the heart.

Idols are attractive. They promise satisfaction in the form of entertainment, relaxation, stimulation, and purpose, but they fail to deliver. Only Christ can provide true satisfaction for our souls. The stresses of fatherhood can tempt us to find relief in idols, but this relief is temporary, and it deprives our kids of the present father they deserve. By looking to Christ for rest, satisfaction, and fulfillment, we can put idolatry to death and give our kids the gift of a present, engaged dad.

Reflection Questions for Prayer

What do you spend your free time doing? What is on your mind most often? Our actions reveal our emotions. Do you love these things more than God?

How is your idol affecting your parenting?

"

We can put idolatry to death

and give our kids the gift of

a present, engaged dad.

Balancing Priorities

Philippians 4:19

1 Timothy 5:8

Work has always been a good thing. Even before the Fall, God gave Adam work to do in the garden of Eden (Genesis 2:15). It was only after the Fall that work became painful and tiresome (Genesis 3:17–19). Yet, despite the fact that work can be difficult, working hard is a point of pride for many men. We value working hard and providing for our families. For many of us, though, this responsibility becomes an idol. How many people have you heard describe their dad as hard-working rather than as a man of God who was loving and nurturing?

Many fathers work extra-long hours to provide comfort and well-being for their families and, as a result, are absent from the lives of their children. It is hard to disciple your kids and pass spiritual truths on to them if you are like ships passing in the night. But that is not to say that we should not work hard to provide for our families. As a matter of fact, the Bible commands it. First Timothy 5:8 says that "if anyone does not provide for his own family, especially for his own household, he has denied the faith and is worse than an unbeliever." God takes very seriously the responsibilities that Christians have for their family members, so the act of providing is God-honoring and good.

But at what point does work shift from being God-honoring to becoming an idol? At what point are we trusting more in our own ability to provide than we are in God's? After all, God has promised to provide for all of our needs (Philippians 4:19). Here are some red flags to consider when trying to evaluate whether you might have disordered priorities around work:

- First, are you working overtime to provide your family with excess? There is a difference between working to provide and overworking to chase materialism. If you are working sixty or seventy hours a week so that you can afford a boat or an expensive car but rarely spend significant time with your kids, then you may be idolizing comfort or materialism.

- Second, do you find your identity in your work? Are you quick to tell people what you do rather than who you are? For many men, their purpose is synonymous with their work. But our work and our attitude toward it should be a reflection of the greater purpose to which God has called us: to love Him and make Him known.

- Finally, are you working overtime to escape responsibilities at home? Anyone who has had infants or toddlers knows that parenting can be trying and exhausting. It can be really easy to tell your spouse that you need to work longer when, in reality, you just want a break from the stress of tantrums. No, parenting is not for the faint of heart. But it is a privilege to be present and point our children to Christ. It is not a responsibility to be shirked.

God has blessed us with the opportunity to work, and we should work hard to provide for our families. But we should trust in God with the same veracity. He has promised to meet all of our needs, and He will do so according to His glorious riches in Christ Jesus (Philippians 4:19). By working hard and trusting in the Lord to provide for our needs, we can model both obedience and trust in Him for our children.

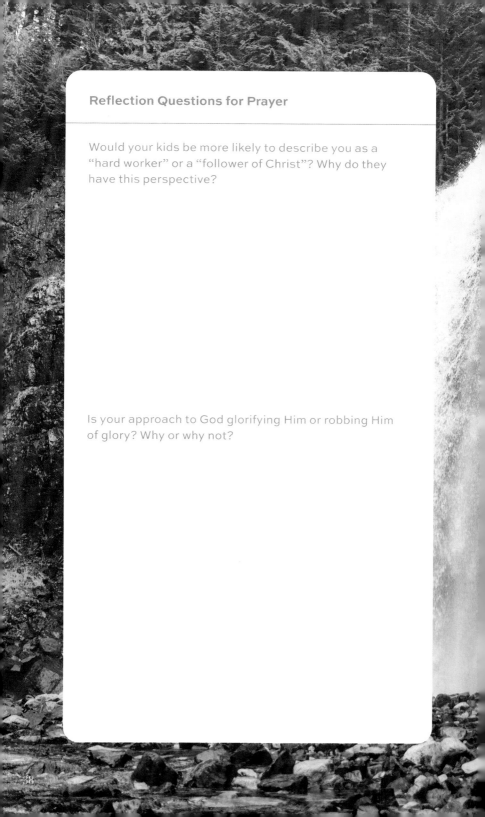

Reflection Questions for Prayer

Would your kids be more likely to describe you as a "hard worker" or a "follower of Christ"? Why do they have this perspective?

Is your approach to God glorifying Him or robbing Him of glory? Why or why not?

"

It is a privilege to be present and

point our children to Christ.

Dealing with Them Tenderly

Ephesians 6:4

Matthew 11:29

"That was terrible! Are you blind? How did you let that kid get past you?"

You've probably sat in the stands of a youth sporting event and heard some demeaning dad yell at their kid for a poor performance. Or maybe that dad is you. Unfortunately, fathers who yell at their kids are not rare. Fathers who criticize their kids are a dime a dozen. Fathers who exasperate their children are as prolific as unfulfilled political campaign promises. But fathers who deal with their children tenderly, now those are rare birds. But why?

Western culture has, for generations, taught men to hide their emotions, to ignore their feelings, and to "suck it up, buttercup." This "tough man" narrative has led many of us to believe that being a good dad involves setting unreachable standards and responding in criticism and harshness. But as is true of many culturally informed per-spectives, Christ's kingdom is different. Christ calls fathers to model His own heart (Matthew 11:29) and treat their children with gentleness, kindness, and tenderness.

Ephesians 6:4 drives this concept home for us. Paul writes, "Fathers, don't stir up anger in your children, but bring them up in the training and instruc-tion of the Lord." The Greek word translated here as "bring them up" is also translated as "nourish" in many cases, including in Ephesians 5:29 (ESV). Reformer John Calvin runs with the idea of "nourishing" and translates the phrase as "let them be kindly cherished." He is convinced that, in this context, it conveys the idea of treating your kids with gentleness and friendliness.

The idea of kindly cherishing your children as you bring them up in the training and instruction of the Lord lies in contrast to "stir[ring] up anger in your children." Harsh and critical speech and discipline often demoralize children and can lead them to further disobedience and obstinance. You've likely seen this reaction in yourself. When someone yells at you, the typical response is to meet that aggression with stronger aggression. Why would we expect children to respond differently, especially when their emotions and mental capacity to deal with those emotions are not yet fully developed?

On the flip side, gentle and humble instruction from an accessible father "keeps children in reverence for their parents, and increases the readiness and cheerfulness of their obedience" (Calvin, 213). Gentle instruction uses a loving tone of voice, is given with a smile of hope, and comes from a heart that has been transformed by the Spirit.

This may sound counterintuitive, especially if you are used to ruling with an iron fist, but that is only because God's way is reflective of His perfect attributes rather than our brokenness. Jesus is "gentle and lowly in heart" (Matthew 11:29, ESV). He is a meek and humble King. He is not One who treats His people with harshness. He does not criticize His followers. He is not aloof and easily irritated. Our natural response to our kids may be to berate them or be overly demanding of them, but through the power of the Spirit, we can exercise the same gentleness and meekness to them that Christ has expressed to us. Treating your children with an attitude of tenderness may seem quite unnatural, but it is the most Christlike thing you can do as a father.

Reflection Questions for Prayer

Think about your upbringing. Are your memories characterized by tender love or harsh treatment? Has your current approach to parenting been affected by the way you were brought up?

What are some practical steps you could take to treat your children tenderly, especially when they are disobedient?

"

Christ calls fathers to model

His own heart (Matthew 11:29)

and treat their children

with gentleness, kindness,

and tenderness.

Lead Your Kids

Deuteronomy 6:4–7

It is easy to think of life in terms of compartments. We go to church for a couple of hours each week. We work forty hours a week. We go to soccer games, and we have time for family devotions before everyone goes to bed. It is a neat and tidy schedule. There is a specific time for everything. But family discipleship should not be relegated to just a couple of tidy time slots. It is an organic practice that should permeate everything we do.

This life-encompassing approach to discipleship has long been a routine practice for God's people. We can see this in the way Moses taught the importance of family discipleship to God's people. In Deuteronomy 6:4–5, He gives them a basic confession of faith followed by a foundational yet simple command: "The LORD our God, the LORD is one. Love the LORD your God with all your heart, with all your soul, and with all your strength."

Our God is totally unique. There is no God but Him. He alone is worthy of our worship and affection, and we are to love Him with our entire being. It is only after we understand the nature of God and have turned our own dispositions toward Him that we can act in obedience to Him.

Is it a coincidence that in verse 7 — immediately after the command to "love the LORD your God with all your heart" — God tells the Israelites they are to repeat the words of the Lord to their children? Of course not. God does not do anything by accident. He knows that parents are in the best position to impress spiritual truths upon their children. He values family discipleship and recognizes that discipleship is not accomplished best in a formal classroom but rather "when you sit in your house and when you walk along the road, when you lie down and when you get up" (Deuteronomy 6:7). Discipleship occurs best throughout the natural rhythms of life.

As Christ-centered parents, we have a responsibility to not only teach the truths of Scripture to our children but to show them how we "walk in him" (Colossians 2:6) every minute of every day. Our children are watching us. They notice when we prioritize the Word of God. They hear us when we pray. They know when we are being kind and when we are not. They know whether our joy is found in the Lord or whether it comes and goes like the wind. It does not take long for our kids to know what we value. Will they know that we value Christ above all? Or will they just know that we make a regularly scheduled appearance at church every Sunday? The difference is often in the day-in, day-out rhythms of discipleship. There is nothing more important you can do for the spiritual growth of your children than to love God with all your being and invite them to witness the overflow of that love in daily life.

Reflection Questions for Prayer

Is your current approach to discipleship one of a few "tidy time slots," or does it happen moment by moment? We need both regularly scheduled time in worship and daily discipleship. Are you lacking in one or the other? How might you lead your kids better in this area?

List the ways that your children are seeing you follow Christ.

"

It does not take long for

our kids to know what we

value. Will they know that

we value Christ above all?

Day-by-Day Discipleship

Psalm 78:5–8

Proverbs 22:6

The alarm goes off at 5:45 a.m. By 6:30, you've taken a shower, prepared for the day, and sat down with a hot cup of coffee. From 6:30 to 7:00, you spend time with the Lord. Then, you scramble to help get the kids ready for school. By 7:30, you are out the door on the way to work. You arrive at work at 8:00 and work diligently until 4:30 p.m. You rush to pick up your kids from after-school practice and stop to pick up milk on your way home. You attempt to entertain your kids so that your wife can have some peace and quiet while making dinner. After a dinner filled with complaints about "yucky broccoli" and spilled milk, you herd the kids toward the bathroom to begin the evening routine: bath, brush teeth, books, and…Bible time? Nope, not tonight. Tonight, one kid elbowed another during books, and a wrestling match ensued.

Every family and every father has a rhythm. How can you leverage that rhythm to disciple your children? By making sure that your rhythms reflect your priorities. If you do not already have time for intentional discipleship and community with other believers built into your rhythms, make it happen. Join other believers for worship each week. Be committed to a small group of believers who can sharpen you and point you to Christ. Create a regular time each day when you gather around the Bible as a family, listen to God speak, respond in humility, and pray together. When our rhythms reflect our love for God, our kids will notice.

It is well-known that kids learn a lot by simply watching. You likely did not give your children a lesson on how to open a door using the door knob. But by the time they were two, they were reaching for every knob in the house and attempting to turn it—all because they watched you. Kids are watching how we live as disciples of Christ, as well. They will notice if worship is only a once-a-week activity—like soccer games—just as they will notice if worship creates the cadence for all their other routines.

Not only will kids observe the structure of your family rhythms, but they will observe how you conduct yourself within those rhythms. It is good to tell your kids that you cannot play quite yet because you are spending some time reading God's Word. It is good for your kids to see you pray throughout the day—not just at dinner time. It is good for your kids to be around while you have spiritual conversations with your spouse or a friend. It is good for them to see you repent after getting irritated by another driver on the road. When they see you obeying Christ, they learn that following Christ is not just about attending church once a week. Rather, it is about living for Him.

Bible time may regularly give way to fists and tears, but if you intentionally build your family's rhythms around Christ and model following Him in all that you do, those disruptions don't matter. Missing church because someone in the family is sick will not mean that your kids do not get to hear about Jesus for the next two weeks. Intentional rhythms that reflect our commitment to Christ allow us to regularly remind our kids of the gospel and disciple our kids day by day.

Reflection Questions for Prayer

Think about the rhythms of your family. Do they reflect your priorities?

What changes in your rhythms might need to be made?

"

Intentional rhythms that reflect

our commitment to Christ

allow us to regularly remind

our kids of the gospel.

What Do I Say?

Ephesians 4:25–32

1 Thessalonians 5:11

Philemon 4–6 (NASB)

If you have ever had a toddler, you have likely gone through the "curious" stage.

"Dad, why do sloths hang upside down?"

"Why does Grandma smell funny?"

"Tell me something I don't know."

"Did you ever have to eat peas when you were little?"

"Which is your favorite Barbie®?"

The questions kids ask and the conversations they start keep parents on their toes. It's hard to anticipate what their little hearts and minds are going to think up next. Because of this, one of the most important skills to develop for a gospel-centered father can also be one of the most challenging. It is the ability to take everyday conversations with your children and use them to remind your kids of their need for Christ and the hope that can be found in Him.

As we discussed earlier in this booklet, family time centered around the Word — in which you listen to God speak, respond in humility, and pray together as a family — is essential. But those few minutes should not be the only time that you talk to your kids about Christ. We should be looking for opportunities throughout the day to share the truths of God's Word with our children. It will take some experience and thought to be able to notice and capitalize on these opportunities, but with the help of the Spirit, you can lead gospel-centered conversations —whether those happen while taking a hike together, separating kids who are at each other's throats, or telling your kids why Grandma smells funny.

One of the easiest ways to have gospel-centered conversations with your kids is to observe them and connect their behavior back to the cross. For example, if they are angry with their sibling, you could remind them that God is patient with them. In His grace, He has given them time to respond to the gospel, so they, too, should extend patience to those around them. If they lie to you, you might remind them that we all lie because we are inclined to sin, but if we place our faith in Christ, we will be forgiven. If they attempt to cover up their sin, you might recount to them how Adam and Eve hid from God in shame after they sinned and point them to the One who can provide everlasting freedom.

If your kids are believers, you can make even more specific applications. If they are afraid, you can remind them that God is with them. If they are joyful, you can remind them that all good things come from God, and we should thank Him for those things that bring us joy. If they have been picked on at school, you can remind them that their identity is in Christ as a child of God (Romans 8:14–17).

Let's close with an important note of caution. There are a lot of biblical truths that we want to instill in our children (Ephesians 6:4). We want our younger children to conform to God's revealed will, but at the same time, we do not want to train our children to simply be moral conformists. For kids who have yet to be born again, you want your conversations to make it clear that the moral expectations you are holding them to are God's commands—His law. They are not just your rules or society's rules. They are God's rules. This will help them realize that God has a standard for life that they cannot keep. It will remind them of their fallenness and provide them an opportunity to think about their need for a Savior, which is the hope for every conversation.

Reflection Questions for Prayer

Speaking to your kids in regular conversation about the gospel requires familiarity with it. How would you describe the gospel to someone who has never heard the good news?

What are some benefits of the gospel that you experience on a daily basis?

"

We should be looking for
opportunities throughout
the day to share the truths of
God's Word with our children.

Connecting with Your Kids

Philippians 2:3–4

One of the most special experiences you can have as a dad is to come home and be greeted by the sight of your little kids running toward you, arms wide open, smiling ear to ear as they yell, "Daddy's home!" It does not get much better than that. Your kids love you and are excited to spend time with you after a time of separation. Kids desire the love and attention of their parents, and one of the greatest gifts that you can give them as a father is to selflessly and intentionally spend time with them.

Paul reminds us in Philippians 2:3–4 that one of the marks of someone who follows Christ is that he "look[s] not to his own interests, but rather to the interests of others." This means putting the needs of others before your own self-interests. There are constantly things vying for your attention: urgent emails that need to be answered, overgrown grass that needs to be cut, the kid's ministry at church always needs volunteers, and you have a tee time. All of these schedule-fillers feel important, but none are more important than your kids. If you prioritize time with your kids, you will find time to work on everything else—but if you don't, it will get pushed to the margins or off the calendar altogether.

Your kids *need* you to be engaged. They need to know that their father cares for them, loves them, and wants to be with them. In many senses, a child's view of their earthly father will inform their view of their heavenly Father. So spending intentional time with your kids should not be a seldom occurrence. In the kingdom of Christ, fathers should be actively engaged in the lives of their children.

On a practical note, one of the most powerful ways to connect with your kids is to take an interest in the things that they are interested in. If they enjoy dinosaurs, pretend you are a T-Rex. If they enjoy drama, take them to the theater. If they enjoy hosting tea parties, put on your feather boa and stick your pinky finger high in the air.

You may not like dressing up as a princess, and you may not like cheering for the rival of your favorite football team when your daughter goes there for college, but that is the nature of love (1 John 3:16–18). It is sacrificial. Jesus was not looking forward to going to the cross. As a matter of fact, He asked the Father if He was willing to "remove this cup from [Him]" (Luke 22:42, NASB). But He made the ultimate sacrifice, considering others as more important than Himself. When you sacrifice your pride, your time, and your desires in order to engage with your children, you are giving them the priceless gift of your presence.

Reflection Questions for Prayer

How are you engaging with your kids each week?
Each day?

Write down some new ways that you could connect
intentionally with each of your kids.

"

In the kingdom of Christ, fathers

should be actively engaged in

the lives of their children.

A New Heart, Not Moralism, Is the Goal

Ezekiel 36:26–27

1 John 5:1–5

Note: The majority of this entry was originally published in 2023 in *Gospel at Home*™, issue 1.

Do any of the following phrases sound familiar?

"If you clean your room, you can play on the iPad."

"If you finish your schoolwork, you can have another snack."

"If you don't finish your dinner, you won't be able to have dessert."

These phrases and countless ones like them are uttered by well-meaning parents each day, and for good reason: they produce short-term results. As parents, we want to have well-behaved, obedient children who do not push our buttons. And we are inclined to implement whatever fixes we can to produce children who are polite, obedient, patient, caring, and well-behaved. So we implement consequences when our children misbehave, we incentivize good behavior with sticker charts, and sometimes, we succumb to frustration and stray into unhealthy disciplinary tactics—like yelling—to try and scare them into obedience. But is that really the goal of parenting? Are we supposed to "fix" all the behavioral problems of our children so that they turn out to be upstanding citizens?

Now, healthy consequences and incentives are often good and helpful tools in parenting, but alone, they can only produce "moral" children who follow the rules. You may "fix" a lot of behavioral problems, but you have not fixed the root of all their problems: a sinful heart.

The Bible describes the condition of the heart for us in several places. In Ezekiel 36:26, God describes us as having a "heart of stone." Then, in Jeremiah, He tells us that "the heart is more deceitful than anything else, and *incurable*—who can understand it?" (Jeremiah 17:9, emphasis added). Did you catch that? The heart is like a stone; it is unresponsive, cold, and incurable. That may feel like a punch in the gut to those of us who have an innate desire to fix things. Our children, whom we love so much, have hearts that are wicked and incurable. No amount of hard work and good intentions on our part can fix that problem. Apart from God, all of our efforts to bring about obedience produce no real spiritual good. Our efforts may bring about behavioral changes, but our children's good behavior is nothing but a façade hiding a sinful core.

The good news is that there is something God can do about it. In that same passage in Ezekiel 36, God says, "I will give you a new heart and put a new spirit within you; I will remove your heart of stone and give you a heart of flesh" (verse 26). Heart change is God's business. It is a work that only He can do (1 John 5:1). Through His grace, He calls people to believe in the gospel of Jesus Christ. It is only through belief in the gospel that lives are changed and hearts are transformed (1 John 5:1–5).

This should not be discouraging for us; it should serve to reorient our thinking. For Christian parents, well-behaved kids are not the goal. Moral kids are not the goal. Even obedient children are not the goal. The goal is to point our children to the only One who is capable of bringing about heart change: God.

We can point our children to God by serving as vessels of the gospel message. God uses people who declare the gospel to accomplish this heart work. Through their declaration, He calls people to Himself in such a way that they respond with saving faith (Romans 10:14).

So, as a gospel-centered father, your main goal is to look for opportunities to point your children toward Christ. Every fit of anger, every lie, every act of disobedience, every yelling match, and even every compliant action is an opportunity to point our children to the hope of the gospel and their need for Christ. These daily difficulties can serve as reminders—not that we are failing to fix our kids but that both we and our children are sinners in need of grace.

Reflection Questions for Prayer

Think about the spiritual state of each of your children. Have they come to know Jesus as their Lord and Savior? Write a prayer for each of your children, asking God to transform their hearts and minds.

Think about your daily parenting trials. How can you use those opportunities to point your children toward Christ?

"

Heart change is God's business.

It is a work that only He can do.

It is only through belief in the

gospel that lives are changed

and hearts are transformed.

Gospel-Centered Correction

Hebrews 12:7–11

It's a Sunday morning. You have managed to keep it together while your kids get ready for church at a snail's pace and complain about every food option you offer. Finally, after third breakfast, everyone is ready to head out the door, and there is a chance you might actually make it to the worship service on time. As you are nearing the car, your son, for a reason known only to him and God, walks up behind his sister and pushes her down. Tears ensue, and you know that you have to discipline your son. You are not going to make it to church on time... *again*.

Disciplining children is necessary, and when done correctly, it produces the "fruit of righteousness" (Hebrews 12:11). There are a lot of practical approaches to discipline, but all discipline should reflect the larger goal of gospel-centered fatherhood: pointing our children to Christ. The best way to point children to Christ through discipline is to focus our correction on the heart and remind them of the gospel. This is because the heart is "the center of who we are... [and it] defines and directs us" (Ortlund, 18). It is in our hearts that we wrestle with evil (Matthew 6:21, 9:4) and experience guilt and conviction of sin (Acts 2:37). It is also where we experience emotions (Malachi 4:6, John 14:27, Psalm 9:1) and root our convictions (Psalm 37:31, Daniel 1:8 KJV). When we direct discipline at the heart, we remind our children of their sinfulness before God and encourage them with the hope of the gospel.

Here are four principles to keep in mind as you attempt to point your children to Christ while correcting them.

1. Godly discipline is never intended to be retributive, and its purpose is not to execute justice. So you should never discipline your children out of anger or frustration. Instead, its purpose is to teach children what God expects of His people and produce the "fruit of righteousness" (Hebrews 12:11).

2. Ask heart-directed questions before anything else. A heart-directed question rarely asks, "Why?" Instead, it seeks to help kids vocalize how they are feeling, what they are thinking, and how they could have responded in a more God-glorifying manner. Here are some examples:

    - What were you feeling when you told that lie?
    - What did he/she do to upset you?
    - Did your action (hitting them, screaming, throwing a fit, etc.) make things better?
    - How else could you have responded?
    - What do you think the Bible says about this situation?

3. If you have asked the right heart-directed questions, you should have uncovered a sinful attitude that led to the poor behavior (e.g., selfishness, anger, jealousy, etc.). You should have also established the standards that God has for His people. Take this opportunity to highlight this gap and remind your child that they are a sinner who has a need for Christ's forgiveness and the empowerment of the Spirit.

4. Share the good news of the gospel. Though your child is a sinner, there is hope. They can be forgiven of their sins and have fellowship with God through a relationship with Jesus Christ.

There are many different approaches to discipline, and not every approach will work for every family. No matter which approach you implement, it is important to correct children at the heart level, remind them of their need for Christ, and share with them the hope of the gospel (see "What Is the Gospel?" on page 80). By doing this, you will help them to understand the depth of their need for Christ but also the depth and richness of the gospel.

Reflection Questions for Prayer

How would you describe your current approach to discipline? Is it heart-oriented or behavior-oriented?

What might you need to do differently in order to uncover your child's heart attitudes?

GOSPEL-CENTERED FATHERHOOD

"

All discipline should reflect the larger goal of gospel-centered fatherhood: pointing our children to Christ.

Flying off the Handle

Colossians 3:8–10

Psalm 37:8

James 1:19

You started off by giving a very clear and calm direction.

"Buddy, you have five minutes until it's time to get your pajamas on, so you need to start cleaning up your toys."

Three minutes later, no progress has been made.

"Bud, you have two minutes until it is time to get ready for bed."

"I know, Dad!"

Two minutes later, the toys have not been touched, and so you say, "Bud, you have not done what I asked, so now we are going to have to skip bed-time snack."

"No, Dad! I don't want to clean up. I don't like you!"

The next thing you know, your calm demeanor has given way to rising blood pressure, popping veins, and clenched teeth, and you are yelling at your boy. Most of us have been here. Despite our best intentions to parent with gentleness, it is easy to get frustrated with our kids and fly off the handle. Every parent experiences moments of anger and frustration, but for those of us in Christ, we can put aside anger and instead put on compassion, kindness, and patience. Sounds good in theory, right? But how does this practically work in the heat of the moment when you can feel your blood pressure rising?

Paul teaches us how and why it is possible to put aside anger in the third chapter of Colossians. There, he is applying the idea of the sufficiency of Jesus to practical Christian living. In verses 1–4, he sets forth the root principle of Christian living: "Set your minds on things above." Then, in verses 5–9, he says that since we have died and been raised with Christ, we should be eager to put to death those things which are not Christlike, such as unrighteous anger. This is only possible because "Christ is all and in all" (verse 11). He is our all-powerful, sovereign Lord and King ("Christ is all"), and He indwells every person ("in all") who has been raised with Him (Colossians 3:1, 1:27).

It is because of His power and presence in us that we can put on those virtues that characterize Him (Colossians 3:10). We can lay aside our anger and put on compassion, kindness, humility, gentleness, and patience (Colossians 3:12). You may feel like your anger is innate—like you have no control over it. You may be surprised by how quickly it can appear. But if you have been raised with Christ (Colossians 3:1), you are now alive to Christ and are no longer a slave to your anger (Romans 6:6–8). And though it may feel like anger has a hold on you, it does not. It is subject to Christ. He is over all and in you.

So, in moments of frustration, you can turn to the Lord and trust that He will provide. He will give you the wisdom, knowledge, and power (Colossians 2:3, 1:11) that you need to put off anger and put on kindness and patience, even in the heat of the moment.

Reflection Questions for Prayer

Think about a recent time when you lost your temper. What caused you to be upset? How were you feeling at that moment?

What Bible verse speaks to that feeling? Meditate on that verse and ask God to help you in the future.

"

For those of us in Christ,

we can put aside anger and

instead put on compassion,

kindness, and patience.

No. 17

I'm Sorry...

James 5:16

Colossians 3:13

Luke 17:3-4

Maybe you just had one of those moments when you "flew off the handle." What do you do now? Do you ignore it and act like nothing ever happened? Do you double down on your harshness to ensure your children's compliance? Or do you humbly confess the sin of anger to your kids and ask for their forgiveness?

When you read those options on a page, it is not hard to pick out the correct one. In real life, however, it often does not come to us so clearly. It's hard to lay aside your pride and confess where you have wronged another person. It may even seem unnecessary to confess your sins to a child because, after all, "they don't know right from wrong yet," or "they won't remember." But as a gospel-centered father, you are attempting to point your children toward the gospel, and what better way to do that than to practice humility and give them an opportunity to learn about forgiveness?

The message of the gospel is that by grace through faith in Christ, our sins can be forgiven (Acts 13:38), and we can be reconciled to God (Romans 5:10). In response to this great forgiveness, God calls us both to "confess [our] sins to one another" (James 5:16) and to forgive one another just as Christ has forgiven us (Colossians 3:13). When we have sinned against our children, we have the opportunity to model humility through our confession of our sins. And when they have sinned against us, we have the opportunity to teach them about the importance of forgiveness.

In order to most clearly reflect the gospel throughout this process of confession, there are two things that can be helpful to keep in mind. First, be specific in your confession. When you tell your kids exactly how you wronged them, you demonstrate to them that you are not perfect and that you, too, are a sinner in need of grace. Second, use biblical language. By using language that the Bible uses, you are helping them understand how they, too, can relate to God. When you say, "I need to confess that I have sinned against you in my anger," you are introducing them to the idea that all sinners are called to admit their sin before our Holy God (Proverbs 28:13, Psalm 32:5, 1 John 1:9). In turn, hopefully, they will imitate your behavior and confess to you when they have done something wrong, initiating the process of forgiveness.

Even if they do not take the first step of reconciliation, you can still use these opportunities when they sin to teach them about forgiveness. In Luke 17:3–4, Jesus teaches us what this process of forgiveness looks like: "If your brother sins, rebuke him, and if he repents, forgive him. And if he sins against you seven times in a day, and comes back to you seven times, saying, 'I repent,' you must forgive him." This process can easily be taught to children. When you notice them sinning, "rebuke" them. The word "rebuke" here means to "express strong disapproval of someone" (Danker). Essentially, you are pointing out how they have fallen short of God's glory (Romans 3:23).

If your child acknowledges that they have done something wrong, you can coach them to confess. Once they have confessed, use biblical language and tell them, "I forgive you." It's important to remind them of what you are promising to do when you forgive them. In his book *The Peacemaker*, Christian writer Ken Sande sums up the four promises of forgiveness in this way:

"I will not dwell on this incident."

"I will not bring up this incident again and use it against you."

"I will not talk to others about this incident."

"I will not let this incident stand between us or hinder our personal relationship."

Extending forgiveness, even to our kids, is difficult, yet it is the most God-like thing that we can do. God demonstrated His love for us "in that while we were still sinners, Christ died for us" (Romans 5:8), and "in him we have redemption through his blood, the forgiveness of our trespasses" (Ephesians 1:7). In Christ, we've experienced the sweetness of forgiveness, and when we forgive our children, we are blessing them with the freedom that comes from being forgiven. Sin between parents and children, though painful, can provide a powerful opportunity and reminder of the beauty of the gospel. May our homes be marked by confession and forgiveness, both between one another and God.

Reflection Questions for Prayer

Think about a time when you experienced the sweet forgiveness of the Lord. How did you feel when you were forgiven?

Of the four promises of forgiveness, which do you find most difficult to fulfill? Ask the Holy Spirit to help you be faithful in fulfilling that promise the next time you extend forgiveness to someone.

Fatherhood and the Gospel

For I am not ashamed of the gospel, because it is the power of God for salvation to everyone who believes, first to the Jew, and also to the Greek.

Romans 1:16

You have probably heard the phrase, "You don't know what you don't know." Nothing could be more true about fatherhood. It does not matter how good a father you had growing up. It does not matter how much reading you do. It does not matter how much good counsel you receive from other dads. Nothing will adequately prepare you to parent your own children. Each child is unique, each father is unique, and each home is unique. You will almost daily find yourself asking, "How do I deal with this?" There are a lot of practical answers to daily questions, but the gospel is the answer to every question that truly matters. So it is important that, in our parenting, we root ourselves — and our kids — in the truths of the gospel.

The gospel is for kids. Jesus said, "Let the little children come to me, and don't stop them, because the kingdom of God belongs to such as these" (Luke 18:16). Jesus wants kids to experience His presence. He loves them and values them as "worthy kingdom candidates" (Bock, 1470). As a gospel-centered father, one of your greatest privileges is to foster an environment where your kids can come to Christ. Is Christ a normal topic of conversation in your home? Do your kids know that you love Christ and live in daily dependence on Him? Do they see His humility, forgiveness, patience, and gentleness reflected in their interactions with you? As they watch you, do not forget to watch them. They depend on you, and their childlike trust is a God-given reminder that as God's child, you too should depend on your Father.

So the gospel is not just for our kids. The gospel is also for fathers. There will be moments when you feel shame for putting work or hobbies before your kids. In those moments, the gospel reminds you that there is no condemnation for those in Christ (Romans 8:1). There will be moments when you just do not know what to do. In those moments, the gospel reminds you that you are in Christ, and in Him, all the treasures of wisdom and knowledge are hidden (Colossians 2:3). There will be moments when you are tempted to "fly off the handle." In those moments, the gospel reminds you that you are not alone. You are indwelt by the One who powerfully works in you to accomplish His will.

As a father, it is easy to feel guilty or try to commit to doing better by pulling yourself up by your bootstraps. But Christ has a better way. In His grace, He has released us from guilt, shame, condemnation, and striving to be better. He has promised to be with us (Matthew 28:20), and He works His power in us to change not only our attitudes but our actions as well (Philippians 2:13).

The gospel is the power of God for salvation (Romans 1:16). It is God's power to make your child a child of God. And it is God's power to make you more like Christ and equip you to glorify Him in this journey of fatherhood. As you walk this road, may you take great encouragement from the fact that you are in Christ and that He is with you as you pursue His call on your life to be a father who cherishes his children and "bring[s] them up in the training and instruction of the Lord" (Ephesians 6:4).

Reflection Questions for Prayer

Think about all you've read in this booklet. How will the gospel change your approach to parenting?

How has the gospel changed you throughout this brief study?

"

As a gospel-centered father, one
of your greatest privileges is to
foster an environment where
your kids can come to Christ.

What Is the Gospel?

Thank you for reading and enjoying this booklet with us! We are abundantly grateful for the Word of God, the instruction we glean from it, and the ever-growing understanding it provides for us of God's character. We are also thankful that Scripture continually points to one thing in innumerable ways: the gospel.

We remember our brokenness when we read about the fall of Adam and Eve in the garden of Eden (Genesis 3), where sin entered into a perfect world and maimed it. We remember the necessity that something innocent must die to pay for our sin when we read about the atoning sacrifices in the Old Testament. We read that we have all sinned and fallen short of the glory of God (Romans 3:23) and that the penalty for our brokenness, the wages of our sin, is death (Romans 6:23). We all need grace and mercy, but most importantly, we all need a Savior.

We consider the goodness of God when we realize that He did not plan to leave us in this dire state. We see His promise to buy us back from the clutches of sin and death in Genesis 3:15. And we see that promise accomplished with Jesus Christ on the cross. Jesus Christ knew no sin yet became sin so that we might become righteous through His sacrifice (2 Corinthians 5:21). Jesus was tempted in every way that we are and lived sinlessly. He was reviled yet still yielded Himself for our sake, that we may have life abundant in Him. Jesus lived the perfect life that we could not live and died the death that we deserved.

The gospel is profound yet simple. There are many mysteries in it that we will never understand this side of heaven, but there is still overwhelming weight to its implications in this life. The gospel tells of our sinfulness and God's goodness and a gracious gift that compels a response. We are saved by grace through faith, which means that we rest with faith in the grace that Jesus Christ displayed on the cross (Ephesians 2:8–9). We cannot save ourselves from our brokenness or do any amount of good works to merit God's favor. Still, we can have faith that what Jesus accomplished in His death, burial, and resurrection was more than enough for our salvation and our eternal delight. When we accept God, we are commanded to die to ourselves and our sinful desires and live a life worthy of the calling we have received (Ephesians 4:1). The gospel compels us to be sanctified, and in so doing, we are conformed to the likeness of Christ Himself. This is hope. This is redemption. This is the gospel.

Scriptures to Reference

GENESIS 3:15

*I will put hostility between you and the woman, and
between your offspring and her offspring. He will
strike your head, and you will strike his heel.*

ROMANS 3:23

For all have sinned and fall short of the glory of God.

ROMANS 6:23

*For the wages of sin is death, but the gift of God
is eternal life in Christ Jesus our Lord.*

2 CORINTHIANS 5:21

*He made the one who did not know sin to be sin for us, so
that in him we might become the righteousness of God.*

EPHESIANS 2:8-9

*For you are saved by grace through faith, and
this is not from yourselves; it is God's gift— not
from works, so that no one can boast.*

EPHESIANS 4:1-3

*Therefore I, the prisoner in the Lord, urge you to walk worthy of
the calling you have received, with all humility and gentleness,
with patience, bearing with one another in love, making every
effort to keep the unity of the Spirit through the bond of peace.*

THE GOSPEL IS THE ANSWER TO EVERY

QUESTION THAT TRULY MATTERS.

Anders, Max. *Galatians, Ephesians, Philippians, Colossians.* Vol. 8 of Holman New Testament Commentary. Nashville, TN: Broadman & Holman Publishers, 1999.

Bock, Darrell L. *Luke.* Vol. 2. Grand Rapids, MI: Baker Books, 1996.

Calvin, John, David W. Torrance, and Thomas F. Torrance. *Calvin's New Testament Commentaries: Galatians, Ephesians, Philippians and Colossians.* A New Translation. Grand Rapids, MI: Wm. B. Eerdmans Co., 1974.

Danker, Frederick W., Walter Bauer, William Arndt, and F. W. Gingrich. *A Greek-English Lexicon of the New Testament and Other Early Christian Literature.* Chicago, IL: University of Chicago Press, 2000.

Geisler, Norman L. "Colossians." In *The Bible Knowledge Commentary: An Exposition of the Scriptures*, ed. J. F. Walvoord and R. B. Zuck. Vol. 2. Wheaton, IL: Victor Books, 1985.

Henderson, Daniel. *Transforming Prayer: How Everything Changes When You Seek God's Face.* Minneapolis, MN: Bethany House Publishers, 2014.

Hubbard, Ginger. *Don't Make Me Count to Three: A Mom's Look at Heart-Oriented Discipline.* Wapwallopen, PA: Shepherd Press, 2004.

Ortlund, Dane. *Gentle and Lowly: The Heart of Christ for Sinners and Sufferers.* Wheaton, IL: Crossway, 2020.

Piper, John. "Why Require Unregenerate Children to Act like They're Good?" *Desiring God.* December 10, 2009. https://www.desiringgod.org/articles/why-require-unregenerate-children-to-act-like-theyre-good.

Sande, Ken. *The Peacemaker: A Biblical Guide to Resolving Personal Conflict.* Grand Rapids, MI: Baker Books, 2007.

Turansky, Scott, and Joanne Miller. *Parenting Is Heart Work.* Colorado Springs, CO: David C Cook, 2006.

Valeri, Spencer. "You Can't Fix Everything." *Gospel at Home: Equipping Parents to Make Disciples* 1, issue 1, August 2023.

Thank you for studying
God's Word with us!

CONNECT WITH US
@thedailygraceco
@dailygracepodcast

CONTACT US
info@thedailygraceco.com

SHARE
#thedailygraceco

VISIT US ONLINE
www.thedailygraceco.com

MORE DAILY GRACE
Daily Grace® Podcast